ALL IN FAVOR OF BRANDING

KYSHIRA MOFFETT

*Dear **Busy Bombshell**,*

I am so glad you picked up this book. This is the first step in the amazing journey ahead of you. Your path to building your brand won't be easy, but it will be a lot of fun! Give yourself some grace on the journey as you will make mistakes and need to pivot at times. It's a part of the game and all of your favs have had to do it.

I wanted to pen this personal letter to you to provide some encouragement and a quick reality check. This book is where it starts, not where it ends. Your dream won't come true overnight. Your dream won't come to life if you don't stay committed. Many have fallen simply because they couldn't develop the discipline that is required to become excellent. Are you familiar with the phrase ten thousand hours? It was coined by Malcolm Gladwell in the book, *Outliers*, which I highly recommend.

His theory is that you must commit ten thousand hours to your craft in order to become an expert. And I believe it. I've been working within the world of branding for five years now at the time of this publishing, and it seems every week I learn something new, and every month I'm a better coach and strategist than I was before.

Commit to your craft, bombshell. Commit to your development. Commit to intentional execution. And commit to being your own biggest cheerleader.

For additional assistance and resources, please visit www.allinfavorofbranding.com. If at any time you're interested in private coaching, you can visit www.thepowercollective.co to learn more and schedule your consultation. Don't forget to follow me on *Instagram and Facebook*, @Kyshira, and let me know your biggest takeaway from the book.

XO,
Kyshira

ALL IN
FAVOR OF
BRANDING

KYSHIRA MOFFETT

Part One

Chapter One

Have you considered what you want your brand to stand for? Let's start by defining what a brand is. According to the American Marketing Association, "A brand is a name, term, design, symbol, or any other feature that identifies one seller's good or service as distinct from those of other sellers". Branding is pivotal to making a memorable and lasting impression on consumers. The experience you provide them is essential to your success. With that in consideration, have you contemplated the basics before you've dove into the tedious leg work? The mere feel of your brand is important. The process of it all can come across really stressful if you skip the first step, which is to define your brand.

If you're planning to create an online space and/or an ecommerce platform, it is extremely important to have a strategy in place to know what your brand will not only stand for, but to also know what you would like the experience of it to be like.

When it pertains to an online space, you must methodize the details of your brand. Unlike companies such as *Target*, *Starbucks* or even *Apple*, you don't have a physical location that you can decorate, create an ambiance, and showcase. Pertaining to online, you have to create a virtual ambience. This all ties back to what you want your brand to be. You can't create an ambience if you haven't defined exactly what you want your brand to look and feel like. The colors you choose, the photos you select, and the products you have in mind to share with the world depend on this step.

To get started, the first step is to build a mood board. A mood board is a physical or digital creation you use to display imagery, colors and/or textures that represent what you want your brand to look and feel like. Some tools you can utilize to create a mood board include poster boards, *Microsoft Word, PowerPoint, Pinterest* and more. It starts with creating a collage that showcases what you want your brand to stand for and feel like to future consumers. It will also consist of the color scheme you're leaning towards, fonts and even logo variations as you move forward in the process.

Your mood board does not need to be shared with anyone unless you would like to provide a web designer an idea of what you have in mind for your website. This is an internal tool to assist you with visualizing your brand identity. There's power in creating in a mood board. Personally, that was a crucial first step for me. It's a great stay to organize your ideas and helps you to showcase your brand experience.

It's less difficult to be guided through this process with the help of a professional. However, when you sit down to do the extra leg work for yourself, you'll see the difference in your ideas coming to fruition. The way you want your personal visuals and entity to be displayed will all come together.

In all, one of the first essential steps in branding is to create a mood board! Even if you have started your business, I would still advise going back to do it. There is always time to plan your growth or rebrand to extend your vision. I tend to edit my mood board every year. As I shift directions or add and subtract to my brand, I have a clearer focus and understanding of what I'm doing by tweaking my mood board consistently.

A lot of times, we do things that feel good to us or that sounds good. Because we've become keen of it, we assume our audience will feel the same. We assume they will enjoy it as much as we do. As an expert, that is not the best idea. The customer needs to be in mind during our creative process. If not, you'll only end up creating for you which leads to little to no sales.

I'm going to provide you some components of a profitable brand. These components are imperative and can help you in numerous ways. More than merely being noticed, these helpful components can bring in the revenue.

I'm going to start with stressing the importance of consistency. Consistency is about much more than posting on social media all the time to tell your audience the latest update on your business. It's about being recognized for who you are and what your brand stands for when you show up.

For example, in design, your color scheme, fonts and typography should be recognizable. People should be able to recognize your common themes. You shouldn't show up differently because the platforms aren't the same. Despite the many avenues we utilize to be seen and heard like *Facebook, Twitter* and *Instagram*, you must mirror the same experience for your brand on all platforms. That consistency in design really matters.

You don't want your brand to appear confusing from the outside looking in. It's more than a competition with pretty fonts, letters and color schemes. This ties into the feel of the entire experience that you are dishing out with your brand. In terms of consistency in design, your promotions, workbook, products, book covers, and things of that nature have to be consistent with their overall look. The emotions you are attempting to evoke with your message and colors cannot fluctuate and cause confusion.

Be consistent in what you are saying and doing. You must be consistent in your role, the products you are showcasing, and what you are speaking about at all times. When people think about you, they need to be vividly clear on the services you offer. When people are not certain about what you do, it makes them uncertain about working with you. Being consistent in what you are saying and doing is also how you get referrals, receive push for speaking engagements and overall exposure to your brand. Being consistent in your approach, in your message, and what you are teaching or providing is vastly important.

Be specific and have a niche. If someone was ever in dire need of assistance with branding and how they interact on social media, I would be the one that comes to mind. However, if I was attempting to dabble in everything from accounting to trademarks, my audience wouldn't have a clear understanding of how I can successfully assist them. This means having relating products and services especially for the audience you are aiming to target.

If you're doing team too much while trying to present it to them, it could possibly run them off, leaving them confused. When trying to do everything for everybody while branding, you'll find in return that people will not choose you because they are not certain of what you do or what you specifically offer. They will struggle to understand your expertise and question if you're the best person for the job. There has to be consistency in what you are selling. There also has to be consistency in what you are pushing or teaching in order to solidify yourself as an expert.

It takes them up to seven times to interact and hear the same things before they can comfortably decide to make a purchase with you. That means you need to get comfortable speaking about the same things consistently. Get comfortable reciting matters on the same topic during live sessions or on blog posts.

Consistency can feel redundant at times. For example, when I promote one of my businesses on my social media platforms, I am basically saying the same things over and over again, however, I am saying it in a ton of different ways. It's not only about reaching new people. The same people need to be reminded that what I'm offering exists and that I want to work with them in my area of expertise.

I continue to remind those who follow me about what I have to offer because inevitably, there is always someone who will forget. People need to continuously be reminded of what you have going on. With all they do during their days, their attention spans can be minimal. Promote yourself daily in some form or fashion. Remind people that you are here and have value. Be consistent.

Be consistent in terms of actually showing up. Whether there's a hundred people tuned in or merely two interested consumers, get comfortable showing up anyway. When you're tired or hardly gaining anything from what you're trying to do, are you still willing to be consistent and show up? Everything you put out is not going to succeed and that is okay. Learn to keep pushing regardless of the failure. Show up for yourself consistently, even if you aren't reaping the benefits of your business right away.

Please note that there's a difference between revenue-generating activities and brand-building activities. Not everything you're going to do is going to generate revenue for your business. Some things are just to get your name out there and build awareness. Some of these branding building tactics will generate sales as well, but there is an actual difference between the two. Regardless of which you receive from the activity, show up consistently.

Another key component for having a profitable brand is valuable offers. Do you really know what your customer wants? You have to be clear of your audience's need. Breakdown who they are, their age group, lifestyle interests, and what influences their purchases. These are key metrics needed to define what they are genuinely interested in.

In order to be certain of what your audience wants, you have to do the research. More importantly, charge your worth, but also know how to sell your offers.

Last, but not least, you need to be clear with your communication and the right tools. When it pertains to clear communication in the terms of messaging, don't try to impress your audience by speaking like the expert. They may not understand and you'll end up losing their attention and lose your ability to relate to them. You have to speak to them in the language they understand. An example, if you're working with a beginner in a program you're offering, you have to communicate with them in a way a beginner can comprehend.

Get to the meat of what your customer is going through, how they're feeling, what they are experiencing, and what they want. You don't have to drop a bunch of marketing lingo or business school words for them to understand what you're getting at or attempting to convey. Speak directly to their core! Clear messaging and communication are important. Can your customer clearly understand what you're talking about and what it is that you're selling? If you're taking too long to get to the point, you can risk losing their interest.

Having the right tools and systems in place is extremely beneficial and important. You don't have to spend a lot of money upfront on tools, but you need a way to get paid, booked, and a scheduling system in place to organize your clients and/or events.

In conclusion, the person behind the brand has to believe in themselves and what they have to offer. As that person, you have to be willing to push through, make sacrifices, and be willing to invest in yourself. The person behind the brand can wildly impact the success of it. No matter how good the product you are pushing may be, if you don't fully believe in it, that's going to show! If you don't fully believe in the value you have to offer, it will come across that way to others. If you never invest in yourself or your business, it will certainly be evident to others.

It's a much better option to invest early on items that will have proven returns than it is to wait until the end when you've already spent money on things that don't really matter. It's much more expensive to do it yourself if you aren't aware what you're doing than to hire someone who has the expertise.

You have to believe in the power of professional development, the power of continuous education, and also the power of sharpening your skills. Recognize that you deserve it and that your business is worth it. Your customers are waiting for you. Your clients are waiting for you! In order to win, you have to go back and tie in the components I've mentioned.

Going back to work on the components I've mentioned can be harder than it sounds, especially if you are uncertain of what is next. If you're not really sure of how things should go, you shouldn't go at it alone when you can reach out to an expert on the matter and have a supportive community to guide you.

CHAPTER NOTES

_____

_____

_____

_____

_____

_____

_____

_____

_____

_____

_____

_____

_____

_____

_____

_____

_____

_____

_____

Chapter Two

Are you familiar with the term brand loyalty? Simply defined, brand loyalty is when a customer repeatedly purchases from you. It's their persistent purchasing patterns and behaviors toward your brand. Maybe you have a friend or family member who only makes purchase from certain companies. For example, the aunt that only wears Chanel fragrances. Or the cousin who only purchases lipstick from MAC Cosmetics. Or think of your best friend who only wants Starbucks coffee and puts her nose in the air if even try to suggest Dunkin. That is considered brand loyalty. You should want to create that kind of loyalty for your business.

Perhaps you have a business where you don't have a ton of offerings, or you only have one or two signature programs. You may not have a ton of things for consumers to purchase. In this case, your brand loyalty can also be received in the form of business referrals.

Brand loyalty matters for various reasons. I'm going to provide you three vital reasons. One, it's easier to sell to an existing customer than it is to go searching for a new customer. With the existing customer, there is already trust in place. You have already established a rapport with this customer. Therefore, you hardly have to pitch anything new to them. They are aware of what to expect from you and will be sure to support your new content.

Next, brand loyalty matters because it is going to increase the average a customer spends in your business life cycle. Instead of trying to target a ton of new people to pitch a new product, you should focus on building a life cycle for your faithful consumers to seek your upgraded product consistently.

Finally, brand loyalty solidifies your spot to a person as an expert in a saturated industry. Every industry is saturated, however, you have to ponder ways you plan to stand out and ways you will bind yourself as the go-to expert that people need to work with.

Obtaining brand loyalty should be a core part of your marketing plan year-round. This isn't a one-time deal or something that needs to be focused on in the beginning of your journey. You should also be consistent with obtaining this. You'll become comfortable and confident in knowing you've built this loyalty around your brand. This is going to encourage people to want to make the decision to purchase and persistently work with you.

Building brand loyalty can seem like a tedious process. One way you can build your brand loyalty is by posting high quality content on a consistent basis. It's up to you on what type of content that is. For some of us, that would fall under blog posts or videos. For others, it could be podcasts or email marketing. There's a wide variety of content one can provide. Whatever outlets you are settled on, there needs to be high quality content provided to your audience to build brand loyalty.

You can also build brand loyalty by clear messaging. Is it clear what your value is? What makes you different? What solution will your products offer the consumers who are interested? Make your answers clear so they are always aware of your services.

A big way to stand out in an industry that is flooded and saturated is actually being available and being consistent. You have to show up! If there are many others offering similar services to you and they are populating more than you on the timeline of a consumer, you will not be the first on that consumer's mind. Be consistently present to stand out.

Revamp your technology to better your customer experience. Is your website clean and easy to navigate for your customer's experience to be carefree? They need to be able to find what their looking for without the hassle of struggling to find an answer. They need to know what you're offering by seeing it clearly.

Your photos need to be high quality and your product descriptions should be easily understandable. If the consumer is confused on the basics, it can steer them away in search of someone else who is clearer with their information.

Think about your entire tech experience. In what ways can you better that for your clients? Work on perfecting your customer's experience whenever they are in search of your products and services.

Step up your digital content! Whatever platforms you are using to showcase your content, dominate them. If you've been slacking on this, it's okay. Moving forward, to build brand loyalty, you have to go hard in this aspect. Dominate your digital content while you flaunt what you have to offer, and you'll see the difference.

Show customer appreciation. How can you appreciate the following and support you have at this moment? It's totally up to you and how you will incorporate this with how your business works but think about ways you can give back. For me, it's creating free, informational content to help my following on topics they are interested in. It can also mean freebies, giveaways or Christmas cards around the holidays. Regardless of what it is, showing customer appreciation can certainly build brand loyalty.

Show your VIP customers some love. If you're already in business, take a look at your records to recognize the customers that have spent the most money with you over the last year. Who are your repeat buyers? Think of something special to do for them whether that's sending them a Starbucks gift card or handwritten note. Even if you wanted to offer them a freebie of some sort, merely acknowledge that they have been consistently showing up to work with you.

Referrals matter too. Check into who has been sending people your way. Small gestures like this go really far. The loyalty attached to your brand by acknowledging your VIP customers and referrals will show.

My last tip to build brand loyalty is to engage with others. I know we're in a world of scheduling apps to stay up on a specific timeline, however, you have to engage. Comment back to others and engage by answering questions and talking to those who can use your help. Say hello, reach out and schedule phone calls. There are a lot of ways you can choose to engage with your audience. Nonetheless, have a voice and avoid being robotic. That is going to help you ten-fold.

Authentic is defined as being true to one's own personality, spirit or character. Being your true self can drive your business forward. We mistakenly think that being authentic in business means putting it all out there and being almost too honest. That's not what it means at all. Building authenticity in a brand comes from focusing on what you do best and communicating that in every aspect of what you do in business. When it pertains to authentic branding, it's important to put yourself first. It starts with you. You're the person behind the brand so it's your authenticity that we care about.

I'll be sharing five steps you can do to build your confidence before we move forward to discuss showcasing your brand authenticity in your marketing.

For starters, you have to believe in your calling. Too often, many of us are hesitant to believe that we are actually doing what we're supposed to be doing. We doubt our abilities to run our businesses or succeed in whatever it is that we're interested in doing. You have to believe in what you are working toward. You have to accept that the gift you were given came with a purpose. Believe that you are walking in your purpose and doing what you're supposed to be doing. Conquer any self-limiting beliefs that surrounds you before you can officially get started on believing in your calling and tackling it.

Next, believe in your expertise. Own that you are skilled and talented in your niche. Be okay with showcasing your talent and talking about it frequently. Let go of the concept that if you make someone aware that you're an expert in what you do, it's deemed bragging. That's not always the case. There are definitely ways to do it without coming off as a bragger. However, you have to wholeheartedly believe in your expertise. No one is going to know that you're an expert if you don't tell them. They won't know what you're selling if you don't let it be known. Whether it was self-taught or you earned the education to master the skill, you have to believe in your knowledge and trainings.

Third, you have to also believe that you are worthy of the success you desire. We all have certain goals both short-term or long-term. Some of us may feel the things we want to accomplish are really far off or that it may take a long time to get where we're trying to go. It can come with a feeling of unworthiness that maybe we don't deserve it or haven't put in enough work just yet.

That is something that can possibly be argued but, in the meantime, you have to believe that you're worthy of the success you desire before that success can happen to you. Too often, we want it so bad that we jump headfirst into things before believing we can truly do it and that we actually deserve to have these things. Have a mindset of abundance that stores belief. Tell yourself that you are worthy as you proceed to authenticate your brand.

Second to last, you have to envision your success before it comes. This is where the law of attraction and vision boards come in to play. More importantly than vision or mood boards, you have to literally visualize in your head what you want! What does your success look like? What does it feel like? There can even be a smell and/or taste to it. I encourage you to be motivated by more than quotes. Visualize, get creative and see it through. On the days you are tired or lack motivation, this is the step that is going to push you forward.

Last, but not least, rehearse your prices. Sometimes we can be afraid to charge what we are worth. Stand in front of the mirror and recite it over and over if needed. Scream it to the sky if you must! Practice until you're able to say it comfortably, rehearse your prices, and be firm on what you're worth.

Embrace what makes you, you! Authentic branding one-hundred percent starts with you. Think about your ideal customer and what you have in common with them. At this point, I hope you have completed your target customer research and your target customer profiles for your business to know who to target. Consider their demographics and lifestyle habits. What are some of the things you do or have experienced that relates to them?

To use myself as an example, I coach women entrepreneurs and I help them package their expertise, brand their brilliance, and monetize their online presence. Some things that I have in common with my ideal customers include being a woman. That's an easy one, right? Well, I was also as lost as they were when I commenced my business. I had no idea what I was doing, and I was just winging it. Aside from that, I have my immense passion in common with them. I am very passionate about helping and servicing others.

Also, just as they are, I was really intimidated by the idea of self-promotion. Charging certain rates and getting sales concerned me. There was even a struggle in the beginning of my journey with finding the right coach for me. In total, these are things I communicate in my messaging to relate to my target audience. Having that relatability factor with my customer helps them. Define your brand and authenticate yourself properly by showcasing your personality through your platforms. You don't have to be stiff and rigid, flourish your personality. Tell people your story. They connect more with the person behind the brand than the product.

CHAPTER NOTES

_____

_____

_____

_____

_____

_____

_____

_____

_____

_____

_____

_____

_____

_____

_____

_____

_____

_____

_____

Chapter Three

No matter the content you are sharing, you want to ensure that your graphics are nothing less than high quality photos. Give your consumers the best experience by placing professional photos in front of them at all times. You want to be certain they are photos that others can read clearly and easily comprehend. As previously stated, consistency in design really matters!

Professional photos that attract to the eye can also attract an interested consumer to your business. They'll begin to notice the high quality in the content you are consistently putting out. Whether the photos are on your website or on your social media platforms, they should be professionally presented.

Know the difference between simple pictures to promote your cause and a logo that represents your brand. A logo is a design or symbol that is assigned to your brand to successfully identify your products or what your brand stands for. Your logo can also be a signature logo that displays your name. Similar to the golden arches for *McDonald's* or *Target's* red bullseye, consumers will know exactly what is being referenced when they spot your familiar logo.

Ideally, your company logo is supposed to enhance a potential customer's first impression of your business. A good logo can build loyalty between your business and your customers, establish a brand identity, and provide the professional look of an established business.

Your logo should represent the colors of your brand through the symbol or design. Understand that when they see your logo, they need to recognize the message it stands for and that you're the face behind it. This is different from promotional pictures of simple photos to highlight a product or service.

Simple pictures can be made of awesome reviews about your business, promotional flyers, and even quotes you live by to showcase your personality. Just make sure they are all of high quality to appease your audience. You can put your transparent logo on your photos to remind your audience of the brand it represents, however, there is a big difference between the two options.

Your logo can be used as a representation for your business, however, professional photos and high quality graphics are the essentials to have in place to reel in intrigued consumers. Let them know what you're offering by allowing them to see it clearly.

Again, your photos need to be high quality and your product descriptions should be easily understandable. Put your all into your digital content! Dominate your digital content while you flaunt what you have to offer through professional photos and amazing graphics.

Whether a logo or graphic photos to promote your business or a product you are pushing, you need to know what you want to communicate about your company. Know the nature of your target audience and how you can get their attention with your visuals. What makes you unique in relation to your competition? If possible, display this in your high quality photos. These elements play an important role in the overall design of your brand. Visual branding can help your company thrive.

Another important element to your visual brand is your website. It is imperative in this day in age to secure your online real estate – i.e. your website and domain name. I encourage you to purchase www.yourdomain.com. Not yourdomain.wix.com or the like. Having a clean domain signifies professionalism from first glance. Additionally, it increases your credibility when someone go to your website to purchase your products or services instead of having to direct message you or send you money via cash app.

There are tons of easy to use website platforms such as *Squarespace, Shopify* and *Wix.* You can use these tools to create a beautiful website in days. You can use as much creativity as you'd like on your site but just ensure its clean and easy to navigate. Your prospective customers will be deterred if it takes them too long to find what they're looking for or if there too many buttons.

Regardless of the nature of your business, I recommend having an about section, reviews/testimonials and a contact page. This is the bare minimum content you must have. Remember, visiting your website is an experience for the customer. Make it a great one.

CHAPTER NOTES

Part Two

Chapter Four

The first thing that's really important when it comes to social media marketing is understanding your audience. Identifying who your target market is can be one of the hardest parts of the process. Its also a step that many tend to skip. This is why many new entrepreneurs overwhelm themselves by marketing on every social platform instead of focusing on those that matter for their targeted demographic Once you really discover who your ideal customers are, you'll gain clarity where they can be found.

To gain clarity on your target market, I would first survey your network. Is there anyone in your immediate circle who would be the perfect candidate for your products or services? If not, consider posting the criteria of someone who be ideal for your offer on social media, and survey those who fit the bill. You're looking to understand their specific pain points as relates to your zone of genius, their demographic information and lifestyle habits. You can then use tools like *My Best Segments* and *Think with Google* to go deeper with your research.

Upon gaining clarity on who your audience is, you're able to market directly to them online. When selecting images, you'll want to use those that your target market will gravitate towards. I recommend using images whenever possible in online marketing. People's eyes are drawn to vivid colors and imagery. Consumers eyes are drawn to things that capture their attention with a simple glance. Get comfortable using pictures.

If you aren't one that enjoys being front and center with a camera, you have the option to use stock photos to create quotes and things of that sort to promote your digital brand. There are royalty free stock images you can utilize from different stock sites. There are also free apps like *Canva* that provide templates for you to create graphics of your own.

If you have *Twitter*, tweets with images are more than likely to be clicked on than tweets without. In this case, you'll want to attach photos to the tweets you're sending out for them to be intrigued. This also gives you a chance to add some brand recognition. By adding your logo to your photos will create that familiarity with your brand.

I know some of you worry about going hashtag crazy when marketing digitally. You can go hashtag crazy if you like, however, you have to make sure you're using the correct hashtags. Hashtags are huge on *Instagram* and are suddenly becoming a big deal on *Facebook* now as well. Be sure the hashtags are relevant to you and your market.

You can look at the people who you admire in your industry to see what hashtags they are using. This will help you learn their hashtag techniques to gain exposure through similar hashtags. I encourage you to save those hashtags in your notes to always remember them. By doing this, you'll be able to copy and paste them as much as you need with your content.

Integrate some videos. This helps you build rapport. People can read our content all day, but seeing our face and being able to hear us and ask us questions helps our audience begin to trust us. They'll see that we're real and willing to interact with them.

Video content can be saved for multipurpose. After you post live videos, you can save the video and copy and edit it to post for those who were unable to make it to the live session.

A really important social media marketing strategy that I can't stress enough is to tell your story. People trust people, not companies. You need to tell how you got started. Tell people why you're passionate about your brand and why you do what you do. What's the meaning behind your product? Get personal and let them know how you got started.

It helps people find common ground with you.

You don't have to share every aspect of your life, but when you're in a service-based business, people need to feel they know a little bit about you. People need to know just enough to relate to you and build a rapport. Help people feel connected to you and they'll become your supportive tribe. They begin to believe in you and the value you add. Soon enough, they'll be helping you promote because they've begun to trust your expertise.

A content calendar will help you save time and stay ahead of the game. Combine this with scheduling apps like *Buffer* for your social media platform and you'll be on your way to great organization with posting your content.

Pay attention to your analytics, especially if the platforms you are on provides them. Numbers don't lie. Analytics are helpful and inform you of the best times to post. They show you when you have the highest traffic to your platforms. These are the times you will want to post. The accurate times the analytics display are the exact moments you'll have your audience's undivided attention.

CHAPTER NOTES

_____

_____

_____

_____

_____

_____

_____

_____

_____

_____

_____

_____

_____

_____

_____

_____

_____

_____

_____

Chapter Five

Social media can be used in countless ways to convey the brand you are starting to build. First, you will need awesome graphics. Pictures that are very enticing and high quality receive the most attention. Photos that are enticing to the eye will attract consumers and make them interested to look into what you are offering and have going on. You have the option to hire a professional to take care of this aspect for you or you can utilize sites with design templates like *Canva* to learn how to tackle these high-end graphics on your own.

If you have a business or some sort of side hustle, you should have a *Facebook* business page. This is a page that consumers would have to officially like to show their interest instead of adding your personal page as a friend. *Facebook* prefers you to have a business page rather than having your audience interact and do business with you on your personal profile. They prefer your business page to be your sole point of business.

On your business page, you will have a header section. This is one of the first things people will see when visiting your business page. You want to make sure you have your logo there or some sort of high-quality photo that represents your brand or service you offer. There's a section where you can add links and provide a description along with your header as well. This is the same for the profile picture you choose to use. There are free spaces for you to post along with these images like links and descriptions explaining who you are.

Your business page allows you to have a pinned post. You can pin any post to your page and you can change it as much as you would like. Similar to your header, your pinned post will also be one of the first things a person notices when they are scrolling your business page. I highly encourage you to make your pinned post either one or two things. Make it whatever your current promotion is or an opt in link to sign up for your mailing list.

Facebook has options that you can link to your business page like a shop option where they can purchase your products from there. People are able to check out your services and see the products you have to offer from your business page. You can set it up where your customers are able to purchase through your business page, or you can do what I do by adding the hyperlinks to guide them to your webpage to purchase specifically from your site.

In your settings, you can edit your page and turn options on and off. It will show you the extra tabs you can add to your page as well as all of the options you can utilize right from your business page. Try to have your profile as complete as possible by using every feature visible on your page. If you host live events or will have virtual events, I highly recommended using the events tab on your *Facebook* business page. Same goes for the videos tab. With the videos tab, you are able to have a featured video and organize all of your videos into different playlist.

Having a *Facebook* group can help improve the visibility of your business. You can link your group to your business page to make it easier for your audience to notice and access it. The algorithm on our *Facebook* timelines have changed. Having a personal space on *Facebook* to update them can be a great idea to keep up with your loyal customers. When you link the groups to your business page, it allows you to post as your business page into the groups. The more they see posted from your business page, they'll be more inclined to interact with it and like the page.

The insights *Facebook* provides on your business page will help you keep track of page likes, page views, post engagements and more. It goes into details of growth or decline in your business and interactions and explains overall analytics of your page. Their analytics makes for better conclusions on your post reach whether organic or paid. The insights give you details on whether there are more women than men viewing your page and also the age groups that your page has been attracting.

Twitter is another really great platform for you to convey your brand. They have an opening space to promote with their header. The moment you click on someone's profile, their header is the first thing you see. There's a bio section underneath your profile photo for you to explain a little bit about yourself. With *Twitter*, it is better to post images with your tweets and links where an interested consumer can find out more on the content you are promoting.

On *Instagram*, the bio is most important. You want people who visit your page to immediately know what your business is about. Different from *Facebook* and *Twitter*, there is not a header for you to utilize on *Instagram*. You will need to be sure to place your taglines or some key terms about your business in your bio to express your expertise.

Because *Instagram* is based on imagery, you will need to switch it up between posting content and posting relating images pertaining to your content. High quality graphics, whether you are pushing content or posting relatable images, is important. On *Instagram*, your content has to properly convey what your brand stands for in your photos.

It's important to have fun with your audience. Everything you post does not have to be a promotional tactic or have a call to action. Get them to view you as more than an *Instagram* page or a business that's all work and no play. You can post things that tie into your company while having fun with your audience. You want them to look at you as more than a person who sells products and services. Have them anxious for your overall content with great imagery.

Especially have fun with your personal blogs. Engaging with your audience is a must within your blogs. Fun and easy things you can do include How To posts and videos, tutorials and breaking things down into smaller topics to interact with your audience. You can play on holiday topics and ponder ways to have fun around the holidays with your blog posts and more.

The best practices overall for building on social media is to pay attention to the analytics your platforms provide. You can also check your *Google Analytics* for your site, which is free. Knowing the best times to post and when your audience is available helps your content get more interaction when you post. It helps you understand what networks are working out for you and which are bringing in the sales. I recommend posting every day on each of your social media platforms at least twice a day. For *Twitter*, I would suggest at least five times a day. On each social media site and for your blog, it really boils down to building an audience of loyal people who seek out your content and that comes from pushing out really great and consistent content for your brand.

Building a community around your blog can seem draining, almost like you aren't being seen or heard for what you are attempting to do in your business. There are things you can do to expand your following and to build a thriving community around your blog.

First, never be afraid to share your story. It helps you to be authentic with people. Sometimes we tend to forget that we are talking to real people online. Don't be a robot they cannot relate to. Be relatable to make the feel of their experience a better one. Allow them to build a rapport with you.

Interact with your audience. Don't just post your content and hop offline. Talk to the people who like and comment on your posts. Acknowledge them while they gain something from your content. Get to know the consumer. The more you get to know them, the better you are able to serve them.

Create a *Facebook* group for your blog. In Facebook groups, you can shape the conversation to your liking. Invite your audience to interact with you and to openly share more on a personal level by having a *Facebook* blog to discuss relatable topics. Not only will it be a *Facebook* group around your site, it will become an environment they are comfortable being in amongst your brand.

Collaborating is also great for audience experience. It helps gain camaraderie with your peers. There could be great benefits of you collaborating and working with someone else. Perhaps they are better aware of something your consumer needs. By collaborating, it's a learning experience for you and helpful that you were willing to come together for the sake servicing someone. Make sure the collaboration is equally beneficial and is going to come together successfully for the audience.

Additionally, it will be greatly beneficial for you to cohost or join a *Twitter* chat. *Twitter* chats are great for many reasons. You get to quickly demonstrate your brand as an expert. It'll be on your timeline for the people who have already worked with you and have an idea of what you do, however, it will also be provided to hundreds of others who are not aware of your products and services. There are a lot of ways that social media can be used to convey the brand you are building! You will see a big difference in your interactions and progress if you implement the information I have provided.

CHAPTER NOTES

_____

_____

_____

_____

_____

_____

_____

_____

_____

_____

_____

_____

_____

_____

_____

_____

_____

_____

Chapter Six

Before you can begin to create content for your audience, you have to strategically plan. You need to know what your niche is. What exactly do you do and why should someone hire you? Have you figured out your value proposition? Your content is for your customer, so you have to discover who they are. What are their problems as it relates to your offerings? How do they best receive information and what influences their purchasing decisions? Getting down to the bottom of these answers will better the content you will push out for your audience. Be specific with your expertise and who you wish to service.

Your content should help to amplify what makes you unique, powerful and helpful to the consumer. It's more than being the most experienced, you have to have more substance than that. Before you sit down and begin to create actionable content, you need to be certain what you do, why someone should hire you, and the value you will provide. Content can apply to your website, social media or mailing lists.

Email marketing has been essential to my growth in business for a long time now. The phrase, 'the money is in the list' is absolutely true. Social media is great, but we do not own our profiles. If *Instagram* shut down tomorrow, all of our photos, videos and followers would be lost. Social media is amazing for building brand awareness, engaging with your audience and can absolutely lead to sales, however, it is more important now than ever with all the changes in algorithms that you convert your social media followers to email subscribers.

Why? Well, in addition to the possibility of social media going away, you can build trust in a different way. You can use email to get to know your audience personally, showcase your expertise through well written emails, and offer special freebies and incentives. My best sales funnels have started on social media and ended via email.

I know that you are probably aware of the importance of having an email list. The struggles can lie in actually getting started and building it. The frequent questions with this seem to be how do you get email subscribers? What's the best platform to use? How do you nurture your audience? You need an email marketing tool. There are tons of options out there and I always advocate for doing your own research.

Mailerlite or *Mailchimp*. These platforms are super similar and both have free options. *Mailerlite* is free for your first one thousand subscribers. *Mailchimp* is free for your first two thousand subscribers. Both have automation sequences and landing page capabilities.

If you already have at least one thousand subscribers, consider using *Convertkit*. The segmentation tools are amazing and help to keep everything organized in a very simple manner. Segmentation means separating your list into categories. I can create sub-lists that showcase people who have purchased my products, people who have expressed interest in certain programs, people who have interest in my products but haven't purchased, etc. As you grow in business, these data points and segmented lists will become increasingly more important.

In order to get your audience to join your email list, you have to offer them something. Unfortunately, no one cares enough about our newsletters to just sign up for that. You must create what's called an opt in. This is typically a freebie of sorts that relates to your business and entices your audience. Examples of opt ins include; worksheets, checklists, workbooks, How-to Guides, email challengers, discount codes, audio/video trainings and webinars.

Once you create your opt in, you will then need to create a landing page to offer it. *Mailerlite*, *Mailchimp* and *Convertkit* all offer the feature of creating a landing page with customization options. Once it is designed, you will need to set up the automatic welcome email that contains the freebie. I highly recommend using *bit.ly* to customize the URL of the landing page to make it easy for your audience to access and to track analytics. You can have more than one opt in running at the same time. In fact, I recommend it. It will help you build your list faster.

Once someone signs up for your email list, you have the option of sending them to an automatic thank you page or you can send them to a specific website. Instructions for how to do this depends on your email marketing provider. Build trust by providing valuable information to your subscribers before advising them of your offers.

You can also provide them with a freebie for joining your mailing list. First, you have to figure out what you want the freebie to cover. Identify how you want to deliver the content, i.e. what type of freebie will it be? Most of my freebies are guided workbooks because I like to inspire action. I want to help guide your thinking and create clarity around your plan of execution. That's not to say that classes or e-books won't do that, but I know my audience enough to know what would be best for them. The more you learn about your target customer, the easier this will become.

I use *Canva* and *Photoshop* to create my freebies. *Canva* is free and user friendly. If you want to make your workbooks or worksheets fillable, you will need *Adobe Acrobat DC* to do so. You can also hire someone on *Fiverr* to do this for you. Worst case scenario, you can use *Microsoft Word* to create your document, make it pretty and save it as a PDF.

Now that you've created the freebie and the landing page, it's time to get in front of your audience. You can market your freebies on social media. I recommend creating a promo graphic to do so. Then share it everywhere multiple times. I've even leveraged livestream to promote my freebies. For example, I hosted a livestream called *Must Have Tools for New Entrepreneurs*. I created a PDF download that listed all of the tools I discussed by category and included a few more that I did not mention. That one livestream alone led to one hundred and fifty new email subscribers, not including those who were already on my list and wanted to access to the download.

Please note that your email list can create tons of passive income for your business. You can have sales cycles running passively in the background while you manage the day-to-day aspects of your business.

CHAPTER NOTES

Chapter Seven

Video should be a big part of your marketing strategy. Video has begun to take over our timelines on each social media site. It doesn't take long to stumble across a video when scrolling through *Facebook*, *Instagram* or *Twitter*. Larger brands are beginning to invest more money in video advertisements as well as partner with influencers who can create engaging microcontent. Small business owners and bloggers can also maximize through video to take their brands to the next level.

A video of high quality will intrigue your audience and help them grasp more of the message you are attempting to convey. People's attention spans aren't the best with all they have going on. A video could help them pay attention to learn more about your brand and business.

Whether you're a coach, product owner or beauty blogger, video can help you to reach broader audiences and build your visibility. I will go into depth on a few reasons why you should implement video into your marketing strategy. I am certain video will help your brand exposure.

Video helps builds your brand as an expert. Being able to discuss your expertise showcases your knowledge in a different way. Anyone can construct a blog post given enough time, but everyone isn't good at articulating their insight. With video, you can meet your audience where they are and talk them through your concepts and ideas. You can speak their language and even use slang to get your point across as it humanizes you. Additionally, if you are using livestream, you have the ability to answer your audience's questions on the spot which further solidifies your spot as the go-to person in your field.

Your audience will see that you are available in more ways than one. They will have more ways to connect with you rather than a blog, website or social media platform. Giving them access to a video of you, whether live or prerecorded, builds rapport and their trust for who you are. You are the brand. People will connect with you as a person more than connecting with your products and services.

It allows you to provide visual proof. You can do live demonstrations of how to use your product, whiteboard your strategy, share slide decks and more. This, of course, is dependent upon the platform you are using. But, nothing drives your point home more than examples of your concept. If you're pitching a product, showing a consumer how to use it, and its benefit encourages them to actually purchase as they can begin to envision themselves using the product.

It's cost effective. Due to the rise of livestream platforms, videos filmed on your phone have just as much of an impact as professional commercials. Additionally, your reach drastically increases when you use video as compared to photos or text. Also, the quality of phone cameras has drastically increased in recent years and it is quite possible to create a high quality video using your *iPhone 7* and *iMovie* software. All you need is a smart phone, tripod and you're in business. I encourage you to make videos an important factor in branding and building your business. You will see a change in how your audience reacts to you.

Video marketing is huge and will continue to grow. It is not going anywhere. With that being said, it can help build your brand as an expert and help build trust. Your audience will receive a feel of your teaching style, speaking style, and will be able to connect in a more in-depth way with you. This is especially true for livestream. In this instance, they are able to ask you questions and have you answer them as they watch you attentively.

Video marketing allows you to provide visual proof to your audience and it is very cost effective. Research shows that adding a product video on your landing page can increase conversions by a little over eighty percent. Those are the numbers you want for the success of your business. If a simple video showcasing your services and products can do this for you, you will want to add this method to your marketing tactics. You are fifty-three times more likely to show up first on *Google* if you have a video embedded on your website for your audience to view.

Ninety percent of consumers watch videos on their mobile device or tablet. *YouTube* reports mobile video consumption rises one hundred percent every year. Essentially, it is doubling every year. Apps may come and go, but video is here to stay. Video marketing makes it easier to explain and showcase the benefits of your product or service. For me, personally, I love writing, but when I am talking on livestream or prerecorded video, it makes it easier to express myself. It also makes it easier for people to comprehend what I am saying rather than reading my product descriptions constantly. It also allows you to capture the attention of passive buyers.

IGTV is a helpful tool for video marketing. It has three main purposes. It is built for how you actually use your phone – vertical and full screen. You can watch it through *Instagram,* but I would advise downloading the direct app. It's simple and intuitive. You don't have to search or browse to get started. It's easy to multitask. *IGTV* is curated. This means you will not have to start from scratch when you get started. The people you are following, and those who follow you, will already be available on the app.

For getting started on *IGTV*, you should showcase video content that your audience won't be able to find in other places. Use this to your advantage. You want to be intentional about your *IGTV* content. Be strategic with your content here. Your *IGTV* content needs to be able to sell on your behalf. It should be quality content that has thought and purpose behind it.

You definitely want to use catchy titles for your content on this platform. Be creative behind what you are doing. Sometimes, this is the only way people will be interested to watch your content.

More steps for getting started on *IGTV* is to upload videos that are pre-filmed and between two and ten minutes. With this, create branded intro and outro videos to brand your business and who you are. Reference your uploads in your *Instagram* stories to advise your audience where they can get exclusive content from you. You will also want to create an introductory video of what your followers can expect from your video content. This informs them of what they will gain from your video. Let people know what your *IGTV* will be used for.

Video can really add value to your brand and services. I encourage you to think strategically of what you want to discuss and how you can pitch your services and products. Video should be a big part of your marketing strategy.

CHAPTER NOTES

_____

_____

_____

_____

_____

_____

_____

_____

_____

_____

_____

_____

_____

_____

_____

_____

_____

_____

Part Three

Chapter Eight

Identifying your target audience market is one of the first steps in launching a new brand. However, for many bloggers and entrepreneurs, defining your audience is easy. It's finding them and then creating content to suit their needs that can be challenging. You have to define your audience in the very beginning.

When launching something new or rebranding to move in a different direction, the power is in your hands to define your audience. Begin by creating your ideal customer profile. You may even have multiple customer types depending on the nature of your brand. Use the target market worksheet within the *Launch Your Brand Toolkit* to brainstorm. At minimum, you'll want to define your audience's age, gender, race, locale, income level, and interests. This is important because you'll want to ensure that your marketing catches the attention of your audience. Better yet, you'll want to ensure that the products, services and content you are creating is relevant and useful!

Here's an example of this, let's say I'm a resume writer and my primary audience are those in mid-level roles who feel stuck. If I were to post an advertisement on *Instagram* reading, 'Let me help you land your first job' as opposed to 'Let me help you land your next job,' I'd attract two completely different subsets of the job seeking audience. Understanding exactly who you are marketing towards can make or break your brand.

Engage with your followers. Once you've officially launched your business, pay attention to those who are attracted to your brand. Engage with your followers on social media and get to know them. You will always have silent supporters, but for those that are vocal, listen to them. You are not required to follow everyone on social media, but the more personable you are with your audience, the more loyalty you will build. I make it a point to reply to every comment on *Instagram* (that isn't spam), every tweet and every email that I receive. Of course, there are times when this will be difficult, but my audience at least sees the effort and they appreciate it.

Additionally, you can learn a great deal from the timelines of your supporters. Engaging with my audience in *Facebook* groups and via *Twitter* has provided me with insight to their challenges, obstacles and goals that they have. This, in turn, allows me to create better offerings to suit their pain points. The key to winning in business is selling the outcome, not the product.

Remember to survey your audience. I survey my audience at least once per year. I ask very targeted questions to get an understanding of not only what my audience wants, but of their wins as well. It is important for me to know how my content and products have helped others. Be extremely intentional about your survey questions. As your audience grows and implements the insight you've provided, their needs may change over time.

For example, let's say you're an expert in hair care. Your audience may come to you for advice on how to grow their hair longer. However, once they've actually reached their goal length, they may encounter other challenges. Now, that length isn't important to them anymore, they may ask for your advice on styling, moisturizing or frizz control. If you have expertise in those areas, you can begin to create new and compelling content to keep your audience engaged. I also recommend asking questions that will provide you with demographic data on your audience. Compare this to what your social media and website analytics provides to have a cohesive look at your audience.

Google Analytics. If you haven't implemented *Google Analytics* within your website, please do so immediately. It is a free tool that will help you to measure your website traffic. Bloggers, this is nonnegotiable if you are looking to pitch brands for partnership. *Google Analytics* will tell you how your audience is finding your site, how long they are staying on the site, and which pages are more popular. It will also give you a lot of insight into the location of your audience and other demographic information. Don't shy away from the data!

There is also a free service offered by *Quill Engage* that will send you a weekly summary via email of your website traffic and other information. *Quill* recently told me that I've had a boost in readership from France! *waving to all of my readers there* I recommend reviewing your website analytics on a monthly basis.

Gain an understanding of economic trends. If you are looking to make money online by blogging or building a business, you still need to know the basics of economics. Understanding how the economy and markets work will aid you in creating a sustainable business model. If you are a service-based business, you are a luxury business. People want your services, but they don't need them. Which means, if and when the economy falls, your customers will become more cautious with spending their money. This is why I recommend creating products and services at different price points. If someone can't afford your hourly rate, have an e-book or course that they can purchase at an affordable rate. Online entrepreneurs are not immune to dips in the economy! A few tools that I recommend using to provide you with basic insight on the economy as it relates to small businesses are *Business Dynamics Statistics* and *County Business Patterns.*

Please understand your customer's behavior. I'm a fan of the Marketer's Almanac by *Google.* It is a free tool that will essentially tell you what seasons your customers are more likely to spend money. Many of us roll out sales for Black Friday and Christmas but your audience may be more prone to spending money around Mother's Day!

Once you've been in business for a few months, I recommend tracking your audience's behavior yourself. Over the last twelve months, when did your business earn the most profit? Which products sold the most and the least? You can drill down to which day per week when your audience is most likely to purchase. Understanding consumer behavior trends will aid you in having better launches and better sales.

CHAPTER NOTES

Chapter Nine

Attracting the right clients at the right time is vastly important for your sales. Your brand needs to be irresistible. One vital key to an irresistible brand is understanding that branding is where is starts. Before you proceed in business, you must gain clarity on your brand, your value and your audience. It's about connecting with the right people who value your services, need your services and who will benefit most from your services.

Speak directly to your customer and build a relationship. Do you ever ask open-ended questions to your audience? Instead of posting a direct sale, build trust with them. Taking the time to get to know them and building a meaningful business relationship will instill their faith in your expertise. They will begin to catch your sales and trust your products. Don't treat them as if they are just followers or that you're too good to comment back. Look to build a relationship with your audience so they know that you care about them.

Add value directly to their pain points that align with your business. Be the one they call and reach out to when they need assistance in your expertise. You want to build trust within your abilities. When this happens, your customers will always be able to connect you with the valuable help they need in your field.

Show up consistently in their space. This means knowing where they spend their time. You have to know who they are and where they hang out online. Often, we put too much time into social media. There is nothing wrong with picking one platform and owning it. You must know where the bulk of your audience is to connect with them consistently. Show up in their spaces. Speak directly to them in their favorite spaces to build that business relationship.

Showcase the benefits of working with you. Toot your own horn! Start talking about your testimonials and referrals. This lets people know the work you have done. Share the results that you received for your services even if the service was free. Make testimonial graphics to show people what you have completed and your expertise. People are usually swayed by others to look more into a product or to purchase a service. If you share your positive reviews and showcase what you have done, this gives you a better chance of exposure. Interested customers will want to check out your work for themselves.

Since the industry is saturated and there are so many people working hard to do the same things, showcasing the benefits of working with you by displaying your reviews and posting the satisfaction of your customers is important. It paints the picture that you are the truth and you have validation behind you that has been successful with your expertise. The reviews and testimonials are similar to people vouching for your services because they were happy with what you helped them with. Let people know what the transformation was and how people felt after they worked with you. You want to document these things to share them about your brand!

To get started with attracting clients, you have to be able to get them on board smoothly. If you're offering a service and people need to schedule meetings and/or services, you need a scheduling tool.

You want to be able to easily provide people a link to connect with you and your times without hassle. Some great scheduling tools that I use include *Acruity* and *Calendly*.

You never want to go into a consultation or coaching call blind, so you will also need some type of intake questionnaire. This is so that you will have some information about them organized before you get into the call with them. You want to be able to create a questionnaire. Some tools for this include *Acuity*, *JotForm*, *Google* forms and a ton of others. It's really based on your budget and what works for you.

More importantly, you need a way to get paid. You need a tool to accept payments from your consumers. You can do this by setting up *Stripe*, *Square* or *PayPal*. There are many more payment processors out there. Whichever you choose is again up to you. But for your sales and your business, you'll need a way to charge for your services when it pertains to your digital brand and business.

The correct tools are important for your sales and to book your clients. These tools display how serious you are to your consumers. Being organized and making sure they have the best experience when working with you is pivotal for your sales. From scheduling tools to payment processors down to the conference line software you will speak to the consumer, these tools solidify your businesses end goal to best assist your consumer.

To attract the right clients consistently, you need to book yourself in advance. You do this by gaining clarity on your availability. You can set up a calendar to help with this. Build engaging sales pages and develop funnels that are evergreen and convert. Deliver a seamless sales pitch and compelling calls to action that will intertest your target market. This is where you express the value you can add to whatever they need that you are an expert on. Create a structured client plan for the best experience with you and your expertise.

Overall, you want to be able to have a consistent cycle for people to work with you. The number one way to do this is to tell your audience how they can work with you consistently. No matter how many times you have said it, you have to continue to remind them of ways they can connect with what you are doing. People forget. When your clients are on social media, they are seeing so much content daily. You are not the only one in their feed. Therefore, you have to continue to remind them of who you are and what you do.

There are other coaches, brands and product releases that they follow. They aren't going to vividly remember your exact brand or ad that was posted days ago. They are going to need to be reminded how they can work with you. Even if you post something simple to remind them, it is still a call to action to validate who you are and what you have to offer. People may know your zone of genius with one thing, but are they clear on the specific of what it is that you do? Are they aware of all of your packages and services? Keep in mind that people need to be reminded of who are you. Consistently reminding your audience how they can work with you is important for your revenue.

CHAPTER NOTES

Chapter Ten

We have more time to put into our business than we realize. It ultimately roots down to managing our time and being disciplined. Discipline is a major key in this entire process. By being disciplined with our time, we must also be proactive with scheduling the important things and sticking to them. Too often we say we aren't feeling something or not in the mood to do something. Truthfully, we won't always be in the mood to follow through on a project. If you consistently put something off due to your mood or not feeling it, I question your passion behind it. I don't question your passion about it in a negative sense, however, I wonder if you need some sort of change to occur to get you back on track.

The good thing about discipline is that you can build it. If you've heard the phrase *"it takes twenty-one days to build a habit,"* it's very similar to discipline. It's not easy by far and it can seem impossible. Once you get a routine going and it becomes a big part of your natural, every day occurrences, it will become second nature to you. Pace yourself and give yourself the space and chance to build discipline. There can't be excuses when it comes to your actual goals and dreams.

You must recognize what is draining your energy and holding you back from reaching your goal. Managing your energy and time are two different things. I've learned that you have to manage your energy in order to get a grip on managing your time. You have to learn to listen to your body and mind as you strive to do different things. Energy management is important. Understanding how you can commit is what saves you from feeling overwhelmed, stressed, tired and even utterly exhausted.

One way to manage your energy and take control of what's receiving a bulk of your time is to create positive environments for yourself both virtually and physcially. You have to stop going into spaces that drain you and stress you out. You have to protect yourself. Protecting your mind and energy is recognizing that you have bigger things in front of you that you are working toward. Set personal and professional boundaries and be unapologetic about executing them.

Contemplate when you are most and least effective throughout the day and throughout the week. From there, decide if you are a morning person and when you are most productive and have the energy to complete your important tasks. Those are going to be the best times for you to get things done. This requires a heightened sense of self. In order to officially understand this, you have to know yourself thoroughly to manage your energy and discern why you are not progressing in the manner you would like. You can't successfully map out your day or week without understanding when you are most effective. Get better at understanding if what you are committing to actually makes sense and is worth the transfer of energy.

Manage your priorities. Are you committing a significant number of hours to your craft every day? Think about the sacrifices that need to be made. Are you on social media more than you have to be? Maybe you should wake up earlier to get a head start on your to-do-list. Be honest with yourself on how badly you want this. You'll need to be real with yourself. If you truly want it as bad as you say you do, what are you willing to lose to get it? What are you willing to sacrifice for the time being in order to get things done?

It's easier to get things done when you're working toward a specific goal. Build best practices for yourself. That's what's going to stop the distractions and stop you from jumping on every trend that is not worth your time. Do your best to eliminate the distractions that are going to prolong the tasks you need to work on for your brand and business.

One big component of goal-setting is the reflection piece. It's hard to know where you are going if you don't know where you are coming from. One practice that I like to do is reflect on the past quarter to look at my wins, the things that didn't go as well as I expected and to find opportunities of growth within my business to plan for the future. Every quarter, I go back to review and revisit to adjust as needed. It's very important to reflect and recognize the challenges you face so you can avoid dealing with it again in the future. It's vital to map out all of your responsibilities that you have to execute from your businesses to your job, family and life.

CHAPTER NOTES

_____

_____

_____

_____

_____

_____

_____

_____

_____

_____

_____

_____

_____

_____

_____

_____

_____

_____

_____

_____

_____

Chapter Eleven

Self-limiting beliefs can take a toll on you and your business. Personally, I had a ton of self-limiting beliefs of my own that I had to tackle over the duration of three to four years. I had self-limiting beliefs about my abilities and charging what I was worth. I was also worried about what people would be willing to pay me for my services and expertise. Through the good reviews and returning clients, my self-limiting beliefs were still in the back of my head, holding me back from my full potential. In my taunting experience with this, it took a lot of time, effort and money on several coaches who told me the same things over and over again until I began to realize things for myself. I'd begun to realize that my self-limiting beliefs were detrimental to where I was headed. I am going to save you the time and money by sharing three mindset shifts you must make to accomplish your goals. How you go about approaching and conquering these tips are totally up to you, but they are the three helpful mindset shifts that I encourage you to really reflect upon.

Number one. The most common thing that I hear people say is, "I don't have enough time." It's the easiest excuse in the book. The main things I've realized with time and time management is scheduling and prioritizing. No, everything won't get done every single day, but it's important to prioritize the things you need to accomplish. Maintaining a schedule whether through a calendar, in your phone, or in a planner is helpful. Stick to whatever method will best help you commit to the things you need to get done. You have to be proactive with scheduling the important things and sticking to them. Especially when it pertains to your business or side hustle. Although you may be working a full-time job or going to school, that doesn't mean it is impossible to commit to what needs to get done. You still need to set aside the time to cater to your goals.

Next, stop believing you have to have it all figured out before you can move forward. This is a huge mistake that people latch on to. Often, we get paralyzed while in planning mode. We don't take any action or move forward because we feel unsure of what we're doing. We assume that just because we don't have it all figured out, we can't move forward. We also assume we need to have it all planned out and feel completely content in what we're doing before we make a powerful move toward our goals. We really think that we have to have it all figured out. Newsflash! We will never have it all figured out. The nerves, anxiety and overthinking come with the territory, especially if you are extremely passionate about what you are doing. You are going to fail at some point. It is a part of the process. Improvement comes with trying relentlessly and learning with experience. You cannot get excellent or become a master at anything if you refuse to move forward because you think you aren't ready. You do not have to have it all figured out to get started.

In conclusion, the last mindset shift you have to make to accomplish your goals is to stop thinking you have to make money before you invest it. There are some tools and software that you will need to purchase to perform your job accurately. Commit internally and sometimes that starts with your bank account. You have to invest in the things that you will need for your blog, website and brand.

I challenge you to think about what you're currently doing for your business and brand that is actually making it harder for yourself because you haven't invested in the correct tools yet. You will not be able to operate like that forever. Don't tell yourself you have to wait until you make a certain amount of money before you fully invest in yourself or your brand. Too often, we allow ourselves to be cheap with our dreams and goals. We mask that with the excuse of wanting to see if it will work out in our favor first. A lot of these things are in our way! Ask yourself if you're allowing self-limiting beliefs to hinder you and stand in your way! Have you convinced yourself that you don't have the time, skill or money? Get a handle on your self-limiting release and accomplish your goals.

CHAPTER NOTES

ABOUT THE AUTHOR

Kyshira S. Moffett, MBA is a digital brand strategist, content creator, award winning entrepreneur, and author. Passionate about brand strategy, entrepreneurship, and beauty, she is living her motto "feel the fear and do it anyway" every single day. In 2013, Kyshira founded The KSM Group, a boutique brand consulting firm which equips entrepreneurial women with digital brand and launch strategies to propel their businesses and blogs to the next level.

Kyshira is also the creator of #HERMovement, a successful business and lifestyle blog that highlights ambitious, millennial women on their pursuit to professional success. Since 2013, #HERMovement has more than 20K global followers, grown into a community of more than 2K members on Facebook, hosted a successful monthly Twitter chat which has been featured in EBONY Magazine, and expanded into a YouTube channel and podcast known as The Bombshell Diaries.

Keeping up the momentum, Kyshira shows no signs of slowing down. Adding her passion for beauty to her portfolio of brands, she launched Life of a Bombshell Cosmetics in 2017, offering premium makeup products at an affordable price to women who are movers, shakers and jetsetters! She also published her first book, "Bombshell of All Trades", a planner packed with actionable brand strategies for women who run side hustles and creative businesses.

Kyshira's continuous efforts and involvement have been recognized by EBONY Magazine, Fast Company, XO Necole, CNN Money, Blavity, Empire Life Magazine, and more! She is the recipient of the 2017 Entrepreneur of the Year Award, Millennial Visionary of the Year Award, Pittsburgh Magazine 40 Under 40 Award and the Fab 40 under 40 Award.

For additional assistance and resources, please visit www.allinfavorofbranding.com. If at any time you're interested in private coaching, you can visit www.thepowercollective.co to learn more and schedule your consultation. Don't forget to follow me on *Instagram and Facebook*,

@Kyshira, and let me know your biggest takeaway from the book.

Made in the USA
Lexington, KY
09 January 2019